PRAISE FOR THE FEEDBACK BOOK

"*The Feedback Book* is inspiring. As Dawn reminds us, feedback is a gift when delivered in a considered, clear and actionable way. Follow her incisive, practical tips and stand back as the positive outcomes come pouring in."

Elizabeth Kuhnke
Author of *Communication Skills For Dummies*
and Executive Coach

"Giving good, constructive and regular feedback is like oxygen to people management and we all perhaps assume that doing it well is as natural as breathing. This book shows how much we need to learn and how businesses and the people within them can improve in this vital and neglected area of management."

Stephen Woodford
Chairman, Lexis and Business Advisor

THE
FEEDBACK
BOOK

50 WAYS TO MOTIVATE AND IMPROVE
THE PERFORMANCE OF YOUR PEOPLE

DAWN SILLETT

LONDON   NEW YORK   BOGOTA
MADRID   BARCELONA   BUENOS AIRES
MEXICO CITY   MONTERREY   SHANGHAI

Published by
LID Publishing Limited
The Record Hall, Studio 204,
16-16a Baldwins Gardens,
London EC1N 7RJ, UK

524 Broadway, 11th Floor, Suite 08-120,
New York, NY 10012, US

info@lidpublishing.com
www.lidpublishing.com

A member of:

BPR
Business Publishers Roundtable

www.businesspublishersroundtable.com

Printed in the Czech Republic by Finidr

ISBN: 978-1-910649-57-2

Cover and page design: Caroline Li

CONTENTS

Part Three: COURSE CORRECTION

Part Four: UPWARDS AND OUTWARDS

Part Five: BEING ON THE RECEIVING END

INTRODUCTION

What do you feel when someone says, "I'd like to give you some feedback"? Curiosity, surprise, optimism – or deep dread? Feedback occurs when one person provides their reaction to another on their actions or behaviour. This reaction may be positive or negative.

Think of TV shows where contestants perform and are treated to the judges' pronouncements on their performance. That's feedback – albeit constructed in a way to entertain.

Think of the comments you write online when asked for feedback by a person or organization you've made a purchase from. That's feedback, whether your comments are high praise or profound criticism.

Now think of work situations when someone – let's say your boss – gives you their reaction to a presentation you've just done. That's feedback, and lucky you if you have a boss who has the habit of giving feedback. We can all do with more of it: when feedback is delivered well, it's a gift – and we can only benefit from acting upon it.

But here's the rub: feedback is often delivered clumsily, and being on the receiving end of that can make you feel as though you've screwed up, without knowing how to improve.

Or we might have earned feedback in the form of some praise from the boss, but since it was a back-slapping "well done" in the corridor we've no idea what we actually did to earn it.

What's more, the idea that feedback includes praise may surprise you if your only experience of feedback to date has been criticism. No wonder people cringe at the mention of the F-word. No wonder we make excuses; we duck giving feedback, and we often dread receiving it.

Working with thousands of people in organizations large and small, it's been my observation that feedback is not delivered often enough. When feedback is given, all too rarely is it considered, clear and actionable.

That's why I've written this book: to help you get the feedback habit.

PART ONE

WHY BOTHER WITH FEEDBACK?

A WORD ON WHY WE SHOULD BOTHER WITH FEEDBACK

When Accenture, a major consulting firm, announced they were ditching the annual appraisal, pundits forecast "the death of appraisals".[1] Indeed, several large firms followed suit. Rumours of appraisals' demise may have been premature: the majority of employers in Europe still conduct them, although their use may have leveled in recent years[2]. Even so, those employees that value appraisals say they do so primarily because of the feedback they receive during the process.

What are Accenture et al doing instead? They're tasking managers with giving ongoing feedback. These more enlightened employers are noticing that, at its best, feedback works optimally as a two-way process and in real time.

So instead of the annual stock-take of someone's performance, a key performance indicator for managers is having frequent feed-back conversations. This includes being on the receiving end of feedback from those who report to them. It cuts both ways.

If you work with other people, and particularly if you manage others, feedback is essential. Welcome to your job.

1. EXCUSES
WHY WE DUCK IT

EXCUSES EXCUSES
EXCUSES EXCUES
EXCUSES EXCUES
EXCUSES EXCUSES
EXCUSES EXCUES
EXCUSES
EXCUSES EXCUSES
EXCUSES EXCUSES
EXCUSES EXCUSES

First, let's be clear about what feedback is – and what it isn't.

Feedback is when someone provides their thoughts to another person on their behaviour. The thoughts given may be positive or they may point out something that needs to be improved. Feedback given well is a gift.

Feedback isn't:

- Telling a team member to "shape up".
- High-fiving colleagues for no particular reason.

- Having a rant at someone.
- Saying "nice job!" to someone as you leave a meeting.

Why aren't these examples feedback? They're not sufficiently clear for the recipient, so they can at best cause confusion and at worst result in animosity. If well-delivered feedback is a gift, then why aren't we all giving and getting more of it?

All too often we don't give feedback because we just don't know where to start, what to say and how to say it. We know that someone's doing a great job, but we don't want to come across as a total creep. So nothing gets said. Or we're worried that someone needs our guidance in order to improve, but we don't want to discuss it with them if they are already under pressure and working long hours.

Maybe we're the ones under pressure; doing the long hours, juggling priorities and demands, so other stuff seems more important than giving feedback.

Or we might lack the confidence to give feedback, with our inner critic sounding off, saying, "Who do you think you are to tell Kevin how he's doing?"

We don't get enough feedback because those who manage us and other colleagues might be holding back for the sake of a quiet life, or because they too are unsure whether to say something and how to say it. Or they are too busy.

We also don't get enough feedback because we seldom, if ever, ask for it. We worry about appearing too earnest, overly ambitious and self-obsessed, and not cool at all. And of course many employees don't get enough feedback because their employers, colleagues and managers believe that's what the annual appraisal is for. So when that gets dusted down once a year, well surely that's the right time to have those tricky conversations and until then, we'll let sleeping dogs lie. Right? Wrong. When we make excuses and duck giving and getting feedback, we're missing an opportunity.

EXERCISE

When someone asks you for feedback or offers to give you feedback, what are your thoughts?

I think ....

....

....

Our thoughts typically show up as phrases we say to ourselves, for example: "they're too busy", "I'm too busy" or "I've got more urgent priorities".

And what are your feelings? Choose words that describe your emotions or sensations, such as anxious, heavy, confident, fearful, shivery, tense or curious.

I feel ....

....

....

2. **REFLECTION** WHAT'S GOING ON?

Your thoughts and feelings about feedback are heavily influenced by your experiences and recollections of it, whether as a giver or a receiver. Some of those experiences may have been positive, others not so.

Now is a good time to pause and reflect on your experiences with feedback and how they have shaped your attitude toward it. Just as you might turn out your wardrobe and sort through what you'll keep and what you'll put in the charity bag before you head out shopping for more clothes, it's important to take stock of how you feel about feedback before you start trying out new approaches.

Think first about your experiences of positive feedback or praise. When you've been on the receiving end of praise from someone, what did you notice? What impression did it make on you? Can you remember it clearly? Did you brush it off at the time with a self-effacing "it was nothing" shrug? What about when you've been the giver of praise to others, how did they react? What impact did your praise have on them? How did you feel during the conversation and afterwards?

What do you recall about receiving corrective feedback? Was it constructive or just critical? Did it come as a complete shock, or were you aware you'd fallen short? Was it a conversation to which you could contribute, or a one-way series of statements where no response other than "yes" was expected? How about when you've given a colleague feedback for improvement – did the recipient receive it as a bolt from the blue? Did they get upset or defensive? Did the feedback make a difference to how the two of you worked together, and if so, how? Take time to reflect on those experiences.

EXERCISE

1. **Note your best experiences of receiving feedback.**
   How clear was the feedback?

   ....

   ....

   ....

   Did you know what you'd done right or wrong?

   ....

   What actions, if any, did you take as a result?

   ....

2. **Now note your worst experiences of receiving feedback.**
   How clear was the feedback?

   ....

   ....

   Did you know what you'd done right or wrong?

   ....

   ....

   What actions, if any, did you take as a result?

   ....

   ....

3. **Finally ...**
   What strikes you as you look back at your experiences
   with feedback?

   ....

   ....

   What insights can you take from reflecting on your experience?

   ....

   ....

3. EXPECTATION
DOES ANYONE WANT FEEDBACK?

HOW AM I DOING?

The short answer to this question is: yes. People need and want feedback, provided it's done well and is considered, clear and actionable. What tends to happen instead is that people don't get enough feedback, and when they do it's not delivered very well. Over time, this can become seriously demotivating, as people believe they're working hard but aren't sure if they're doing a good job, or if their hard work is being noticed. Or they may have the nagging feeling they're not quite getting something right but don't know what to do instead. Worse, some employees want feedback to help them develop, but instead they are micromanaged on every single thing they do.

If you're in any doubt that people want feedback, ask a colleague in human resources about comments made by leavers in exit interviews. Chances are you'll hear that lots of leavers say something along the lines of "No-one told me how I was doing".

According to the UK's Investors in People (IiP) latest Job Exodus Report,[3] almost half the employees they polled were considering a job move, and one in three said they were unhappy at work. The biggest gripe to emerge in IiP's study? If you think it's pay, think again. Pay took third place for reasons behind unhappiness, after "poor management" and "not feeling valued". One of the report's recommendations for managers was to simply say "thank you" more often.

People want to be noticed when they've worked hard and done their best. This also applies to abilities that come to us easily – we can take them for granted and underestimate ourselves until someone points out what a difference we've made. And we'd much prefer to know if there's something we need to improve (if we're honest), rather than people talking behind our backs, or the shortcoming stunting our career progress. It's why I have a problem with the term "negative feedback": although it may be tough to hear at the time, the overall experience usually has a positive outcome. We've all got blind spots, and feedback is brilliant at shining a light on them.

EXERCISE
Refer back to your best experiences of receiving feedback.
What blind spots did they illuminate in some way?

....

What strengths and skills were you taking for granted?

....

What improvements were pointed out to you?

....

4. NECESSITY
WELCOME TO YOUR JOB

Feedback is essential at work; if you lead groups of people, you are responsible for their development and performance. Feedback is also essential if you work with others in project teams, if you have a boss, if you work with clients, or contractors and suppliers. You get the picture: if you work in an organization, it's highly likely that you'll need to give feedback to others as part of your role – and you'll need to receive it.

Until recently, most organizations used the annual appraisal to manage the process of giving feedback on performance at work. Increasingly, employers are questioning if this is the best way to manage performance.

The annual cycle is only one of many ways to look at organizational, departmental and individual performance; the yearly appraisal now struggles to keep up with the pace of how firms work. Organizations are now required to move at a faster pace, deliver results both long- and short-term, and be more agile, proactive and responsive. This agility needs to be reflected in how performance is managed. An employee's performance can change for better or worse from one project to another, as teams are formed, broken up and re-formed.

Appraisals can be time-consuming, incomplete (can you really remember what your team did 11 months back?) and at worst, a soul-destroying, box-ticking-exercise. Even where employers retain some kind of annual inventory committed to a formal document or system, there's a growing acceptance that this alone isn't enough to get the best performance from people.

If people want and need more frequent feedback than that provided by the annual appraisal process, we need to get the feedback habit. Your team members (and many colleagues) will expect you to give them feedback on their performance – often. Increasingly, these same people, as well as your managers, will expect to give you feedback on how you're performing.

As you'll see, unlike the annual appraisal, these more frequent gifts of feedback will be short and simple. So "I haven't got time" will not be a valid reason to duck the responsibility you have to support your colleagues' performance.

Welcome to your job.

EXERCISE

Who are the people you need to give feedback to – and receive feedback from – on a regular basis as a requirement of your job role? Clue: there will probably be more names than you think.

....

....

5. FRAMEWORK
GIVE PEOPLE
AN **EDGE**

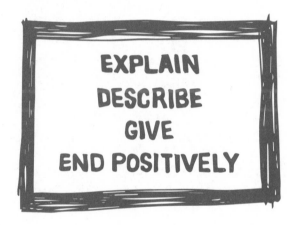

EXPLAIN
DESCRIBE
GIVE
END POSITIVELY

By now you'll have got the message that feedback is essential if you work with other people. But how do you actually do it? How do you deliver feedback that really will be a gift to your recipient?

I find it helps to follow a framework to make sure feedback is considered, clear and actionable. It's essential that the action that has prompted the feedback is clearly identified, as well as the impact it has had. What's more, it's about having a dialogue – feedback needs to be discussed with the recipient, not dropped on them.

It's important to remember why the feedback conversation is taking place: to sustain improved performance, whether that's praising what's good or pointing out what needs to be improved. That's why it's about giving people an **EDGE**.

EXPLAIN using a clear example of the exact behaviour or action that has prompted your feedback. The sooner the better. Stick to the facts and be brief.

DESCRIBE the effect of the behaviour. What impact has it had on colleagues/results/stakeholders? Keep it factual, short and simple.

GIVE the recipient the mic. Invite them to speak and give them a fair hearing, in their own words. What action will they take? What will they do more/less of? If the feedback is positive, it's their chance to take some credit. If the feedback is about an improvement that's required, this is their chance to take responsibility. Feedback delivered well becomes a dialogue.

END POSITIVELY, with your encouragement and your recipient's commitment. Let them have the last word whenever possible.

Next we're going to take each element of giving people an **EDGE**, and illustrate how they build into clear and actionable feedback conversations. But meanwhile, take a moment to consider how you and your colleagues currently measure up.

EXERCISE

Think back to a recent discussion where you gave feedback.
Using the **EDGE** framework, score yourself out of 10 on each of the four elements (10 being the best and 1 the worst)

E.................. D.................. G.................. E..................

Think back to a recent discussion where you received feedback.
Using the **EDGE** framework, score the feedback-giver out of 10 on each of the four elements (10 being the best and 1 the worst)

E.................. D.................. G.................. E..................

Now think about when you want to give feedback; how are you going to start the conversation? I suggest the briefest of introductions. Depending on the person and situation, you could say:

"I want to give you some feedback on that report; when's a good time?"

"I'd like to offer some feedback on that presentation; shall we talk now?"

"Let's talk about that workshop. I need to give you some feedback, is that OK?"

6. **BEHAVIOUR**
MIND YOUR
LANGUAGE

Over many years of training managers to get the best from their people, I've heard participants give countless examples of feedback that were unclear and would leave any recipient utterly baffled about what to do next. Through further discussion, participants often realize that they have been following bad examples (from their managers) as they in turn give feedback to their teams.

The key to getting clarity is what the first **E** in **EDGE** is all about: explaining the exact action you've observed that's prompted the feedback. Once people recognize the importance of this element, their readiness to give feedback increases dramatically – and so will yours.

Before you have a feedback conversation, make sure you're clear on the behaviour that has prompted the feedback. Here's a very quick grammar lesson: to discuss any behaviour we need to use verbs. Verbs are what English teachers refer to as "doing words": speak, listen, take, write, present.* Don't panic: there's a cheat sheet of verbs in the resources section of this book.

You might say (with **verbs** in bold type):

*"You **wrote** up the meeting notes in good time."*
*"You **talked** across the client when he spoke."*
*"You **spoke** clearly and **made** eye contact with the audience."*
*"You **didn't correct** the errors in the spreadsheet before **sending** it over."*

Try this test: would an impartial observer agree with your account of the action that has prompted the feedback?

All too often, givers of feedback succumb to the urge to dress it up and lapse into using adjectives (words that describe or modify other words: good, bad, calm, eager, zealous, etc.). This is unhelpful because the recipient may have no idea what they *did* to prompt you to give feedback, to say they were "aggressive", "proactive", "lacklustre" or "authoritative". As a result, they'll have no idea what to do more or less of. It's also risky because adjectives are your subjective interpretation of their action and can be judgmental. Your recipient may disagree with your opinion, and you end up having a very different conversation than that which you intended.

EXERCISE

Check out the verbs cheat sheet in the resources section.
Highlight the verbs that best fit the action you'll be discussing
the next time you give someone feedback.

....

....

....

....

....

....

....

....

....

* If you're reading this book and English is not your first language,
you probably a) need no explanation of the distinction between
verbs and adjectives, and b) you may be amused at the typical
Brit's poor grasp of our own grammar. Please bear with us here. If
you're a Brit in need of grammatical support, use the verbs cheat
sheet on page 179 to help you.

7. **IMPACT**
CAUSE AND EFFECT

Once you're clear on the behaviour that has prompted the feedback, the next step in the **EDGE** framework requires you to **D**escribe the impact it had.

Your observations on both the behaviour and its impact need to be able to withstand scrutiny. Again, you'll need to ask: would an impartial observer agree with your account of the behaviour and its impact?

What happened as a result of the person's behaviour? If the behaviour was the cause, what was the effect? What were the consequences? For example:

- If A shouted (action) at B, did B get upset (impact)?
- If A asked (action) relevant questions, did B respond with the information needed (impact)?
- If A interrupted (action) B, did B clam up and stop contributing to the meeting (impact)?
- If A rehearsed (action) their presentation, did they handle questions from the audience well (impact)?

Top tip: expand your repertoire of verbs. Get in the habit of noticing when you're thinking in adjectives, such as "she's efficient" or "he's sloppy", and ask yourself what actual behaviours people have shown that led you to form those judgments.

What if you're not sure of the impact the action had? Ask yourself if you're unsure because you weren't paying enough attention at the time – and be honest. If that's the case, make a mental note to watch out for a recurrence of the behaviour. Next time pay closer attention to the impact on a task's quality, timing and delivery, and on other people. Providing useful feedback that's going to be a gift to the recipient requires us to really sharpen our powers of observation, which we will discuss in more detail later.

EXERCISE
Refer back to the verbs generated in the previous exercise.
What was the impact of each action?

....

8. DIALOGUE
IT'S NOT A
MONOLOGUE

The **G** in **EDGE** is about **G**iving the recipient of your feedback the mic – letting them speak and listening well to what they have to say in response. When feedback is delivered well, it becomes a dialogue. How do you hand the conversation over to your recipient? The simplest way to do this is to ask a question.

"What do you think?"
"How did it seem to you?"
"What was your take on that meeting?"
"What worked for you?"
"How do you feel about how it went?"

Be prepared for feedback recipients (even if you're giving the highest praise) to take a moment to process what you've just explained before they formulate their reply. Your feedback may have shone the light on a blind spot, something that they've been unaware of until now. Your feedback may have pointed out strengths they've been taking for granted. So resist the urge to fill the void with words and remember it's not about you – hand that mic over and give them time to speak. Feedback delivered well is a gift: let your recipients unwrap it for themselves.

A crucial part of **G**iving feedback recipients the mic is that you listen and then observe very carefully how they respond. Have they grasped the behaviour that you have pointed out to them? Have they heard the impact that their action had? How can you tell how the feedback recipient truly feels about the feedback they have been given? Is it by what they are saying? Or how they're saying it – gesture, posture, facial expression? You may need a few coaching questions to sustain the conversation.

"What did you notice?"
"What were you aware of?"
"How did they respond?"

Once your feedback recipient responds, they become active, not passive. As they get more involved in the conversation, they are more likely to take ownership of their behaviour and its impact.

If you don't give them the mic, you're just giving them a lecture; fall into that trap and the responsibility remains with you.

EXERCISE
Think back to a recent discussion about performance – yours or the other person's. Who had the mic the longest? What impact did that have on the recipient?

....

....

....

9. COMMITMENT
POSITIVE ENDING

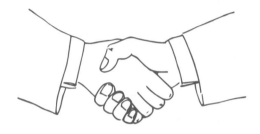

The final **E** in the **EDGE** framework is for **E**nding. It is important to end the feedback conversation on a positive note, with the recipient's commitment to make use of the gift they've been given.

You may need to steer the conversation to this point, particularly if you've done a good job of giving the other person the mic. You may find that they get carried away. The simplest way to do that while keeping the conversation going is to ask another question.

"How will you keep it up?"
"What will you do differently?"
"How will we both know it's working?"
"When's the next opportunity for you to do this?"

Notice that the example questions listed above are all open questions that require the recipient to be specific. Avoid closed questions that can only be answered with a "yes" or a "no" – that's not really giving your recipient the mic. Closed questions are more likely to be commands with question marks at the end, and therefore not what we're after here – a productive dialogue that ends well. Open questions – that begin with "what", "how", "when", "where" and "who" – can open up the dialogue. You'll get your recipient thinking and articulating what they'll do more or less of and how they'll go about it.

I'll never forget a former boss's words at the end of a conversation when I'd received some urgent corrective feedback, "I'm very sure you can do this, and am curious to know how you will – so how will you?"

Listen for commitment and don't settle for "I'll try"; ask what specific steps they'll take. Let them have the last word whenever possible.

EXERCISE

Think back to a recent discussion about performance – yours or the other person's. How did it end? Who had the last word?

....

....

....

As you progress through this book, you'll see how the **EDGE** framework applies to feedback in different situations, whether the feedback is praising good performance or pointing out what needs to improve and how. You'll also see how the elements of the **EDGE** framework build into clear and simple conversations that you can assimilate into what you're already doing on a daily basis, as you build your skills and feedback becomes a habit.

10. GET THE HABIT
SPOTTING EVERYDAY
OPPORTUNITIES

So far you have reflected on your own experiences of feedback and have been given a clear framework to structure a considered, clear and actionable feedback conversation. But there's more to do before you can start giving people an **EDGE** in earnest. Here's a really worthwhile exercise to get you into the habit of spotting everyday opportunities when you can give the gift of feedback to other people.

EXERCISE

Pay attention to other people's actions – what verbs best describe these? (Refer to the verbs cheat sheet)

....

Look at the effect of those actions – what impact do they have and what responses do they get?

....

PART TWO

POSITIVE
STROKES

A WORD ON POSITIVE STROKES

If you thought this book was all about how to criticize people, think again. We need to balance feedback over time so that there's more praise than criticism. This may run counter to how many of us are wired, particularly at work, where the emphasis is often on mitigating risk and we can therefore default to fault-finding. Or you may find the notion of praising people on a regular basis somewhat creepy. If so, consider this: if all the people that you're giving feedback to genuinely need much more course correction and improvement than they need praise, how on earth did they get the job and why are they still doing it? The only circumstance where that might apply is a complete beginner; but even then they'll have plenty of redeeming features that helped them get the job.

1. **PROPORTION**
GET THE BALANCE RIGHT

Getting the feedback habit requires us to get the balance right. We need to give more positive feedback – praise – than feedback for improvement. If the balance tips toward corrective feedback, the person on the receiving end will soon tire of the constant criticism, no matter how well-intentioned it may be.

In *Positivity*,[4] Barbara Fredrickson suggests a ratio of at least 3:1 in favour of praise at work. Workplace cultures vary and some will find 5:1 comes easily; others may find 3:1 a stretch, but you get the idea – we need to praise more than criticize. By tipping the balance of the feedback in favour of positive over negative, you will accomplish two vital shifts over time: you'll take a much less nit-picking and far more positive view of how people are doing; and people will know where they stand with you. (By the way, Fredrickson recommends a much greater weighting toward praise in our personal relationships too).

In case you're starting to feel somewhat uncomfortable at the idea of giving positive feedback, remember it's not about you. Giving positive feedback to people will not turn you into the office creep. This isn't about flannel, flattery and buttering people up. When you apply the **EDGE** framework to giving feedback, you'll be sticking to the facts.

Positive feedback is about giving people the gift of noticing what they're doing well and saying it in a way they can understand and act upon.

Positive feedback requires us to develop our powers of observation so we actually notice good performance, much more often than we're probably used to. That shift in focus and attention can be a revelation for managers. I often hear them say, "I had no idea X was doing that so well" and "Actually Y is great at something the rest of us really struggle with". Over time you'll develop the feedback habit so that you'll be praising people on a daily basis.

First, time to reflect on your experience of receiving praise.

EXERCISE
Think back to your own experiences of receiving praise from colleagues.
How did you feel about yourself at the time and after you received the praise?

....

....

How did you feel toward the giver of the feedback?

....

....

2. DENIAL
WHY "WELL DONE" ISN'T ENOUGH

When I explain to managers in training workshops that the balance of feedback needs to be weighted in favour of praise, a common response is, "Yeah, but I praise my team all the time. I mean, I'm always telling them "well done" or giving them a high five." Well, at least it's better than nothing, and it's certainly better than a constant stream of detailed, nit-picking criticism.

However, chances are this praise isn't quite the gift that may have been intended. The recipient knows that they have pleased their manager or superior in some way or other, but they're not sure exactly how, and even less clear about what they should keep doing to further improve. What's more, if "well done" and "good effort" are the extent of your repertoire of praises, used repeatedly your comments may be received as throwaway, meaningless and even insincere.

Simply saying "great job" and leaving it at that isn't considered, clear and actionable feedback. It's a wasted opportunity, as it's a gift that the recipient can't use.

Instead of "fantastic!" "brilliant job!" and "awesome!", people need to know exactly what it is they've done well. They may have no idea that the way they structured their presentation was what sustained the audience's attention, or that how they explained a complex data problem to a senior manager saved both time and the manager's reputation. They'll continue to have no idea unless you tell them, in a way that's considered, clear and actionable and in a way that will encourage them to repeat the praiseworthy action. Even worse, they may have some idea they're improving, but they may be uncertain if anyone has noticed – and could soon become demotivated. These people urgently need positive reinforcement about what they're doing right.

EXERCISE
Think back to your own experiences of receiving praise from colleagues.
On a scale of 1-10, where 1 = "not a clue" and 10 = "crystal clear", rate how clear you were on what you'd done that merited the praise. What was the action?

....

How did the feedback encourage you to take the action more often that merited the praise?

....

Top tip: if you haven't given a colleague feedback by lunchtime, you have probably missed an opportunity. Or been working alone, without wifi or a phone. Or on holiday. Aim to spot something good before lunchtime and give positive feedback.

3. OBSERVATION
HOW WE'RE WIRED
AND WHY IT MATTERS

The prevailing work culture is just one thing that can hold us back from giving more positive than corrective feedback than corrective. As humans, we're hardwired to pay more attention to what's wrong or missing than to what's right. It's a survival mechanism we've evolved with and it shows up even now. Lost a five-pound note on your journey home? It'll bug you for much longer than the glow of finding another one down the back of the sofa. Resource loss – what's deficient or lacking – packs a bigger punch for us than does resource gain. This means that whereas identifying areas for improvement probably comes easily to us, we all need to work that little bit harder to spot what someone's actually doing well.

Another point about our wiring that affects our approach to feedback is that we all have biases, and they're so deeply embedded that most of us are completely unaware of them. For example, we can attribute our own errors to a whole host of external factors, but when it comes to successes, well (obviously!) they're down to us;

our skills combined with the huge effort we put in. Yet we tend to do the exact opposite when it comes to others' errors and successes: we put the former down to the individual's innate failings and dismiss their successes as mere flukes and luck. We need to be aware of this attribution error when we're giving feedback.

Another way in which unconscious bias can show up is called the "horns and halo effect". If you've ever felt unfairly treated compared to colleagues, or been the maker of unfair comparisons yourself, it may have been down to horns or halos. We can give some colleagues horns when we let a single slip-up contaminate our view of their otherwise promising overall performance. Others may get undeserved halos because of one thing they've done well, when the rest of their performance could bear improvement.

The key to treating people fairly is to sharpen your powers of observation.

EXERCISE

Think about skills that are highly valued where you work.
For example, it may be giving presentations, or selling, or extracting useful insights from mountains of data. List as many as you can. To achieve greater clarity, see if you can rank them in order of value to your employer (and by the way, if you've no idea what skills are highly valued where you work, that's a conversation well worth having with someone – soon).

....

....

4. **SPECIFICITY**
NAIL THE DETAIL

To make positive feedback a gift that benefits the recipient, it needs to be considered, clear and actionable. Recipients will get the message loud and clear about the exact behaviour that's worked well in this instance and realize that they'd be smart to take that action more often.

As the feedback giver, we need to nail the details of someone's actions if we're going to master the first **E** in giving them an **EDGE** – **E**xplaining the action that prompted the feedback. Since we're focusing on positive reinforcement for now, those actions will be the ones that proved effective.

For example they:

"Took time to rehearse your presentation."
"Spoke clearly and coherently."
"Wove likely questions from the audience into your presentation."
"Handled questions well, giving concise answers to some and involving colleagues for others."

Identifying actions will then lead us to their consequences – the **D** stage in **EDGE,** when we **D**escribe the impact. Again we need to hone our powers of observation to nail the detail, paying close attention to the reactions and responses of others. So we're not just watching, listening and noticing the behaviour that's working well, we're also watching, listening and noticing the response that behaviour gets. Here's a clue: you probably won't do a good job of this if you're fiddling with your smartphone. You need to fully give attention to what's actually going on.

A manager giving feedback on the examples above could then move on to **D**escribe the impact of those actions thus:

"The presentation flowed well, was clearly signposted and ran to time."
"Speaking clearly and coherently meant you came across as knowl-edgeable and confident."
"Anticipating audience questions prompted lots of audience nods as the presentation progressed."
"Giving concise answers visibly reassured some audience mem-bers and involving colleagues demonstrated it was a team effort."

Just in case you're worried that giving positive feedback will turn you into the office creep, take another look through these examples of what a manager can say to nail that detail. How creepy do those soundbites seem to you? Not very, I'll bet. That's because they're simple and factual. So if you've been ducking giving feedback be-cause of this, you should have no more excuses.

EXERCISE

Look back at your list of valued skills from the previous section and choose one. Observe a colleague who performs that skill particularly well.

Identify the behaviours. How do they do it? (Remember to use verbs, not adjectives)

....

....

....

....

What response(s) does the behaviour elicit from others?

....

....

....

What positive impact does their performance have?

....

....

....

5. SINCERITY
MEAN IT

As humans, we are pretty good at spotting a fake when it comes to sincerity. We can make this judgment in a heartbeat, even before the faker has uttered a word. Their body language – facial expression and eye contact, posture, gestures and how they're breathing – will transmit signals that we'll interpret without thinking, because we've had a lifetime of practice at spotting the difference between a fake and the genuine article.

Feedback – positive or otherwise – needs to be sincere for the recipient to give it credence, let alone act upon it. That's another reason why "well done" just isn't enough. Yet, like all learners new to something, in this case giving feedback, we can be clumsy as our anxiety to perform well may lead us to overdo it. The feedback then becomes too long, too flowery, too confusing – and uncomfortable for both parties.

To be sincere, it helps to connect with the motivation for giving feedback. Why is it important to give someone this feedback? Think of actors who ask directors, "What's my motivation here?" so they can authentically portray their character. Think about what your motivation is with this person in this situation and the reason giving them this feedback is important. For example, you may be motivated to give someone positive feedback because you:

- Believe that good effort should be recognized
- Want to encourage a new team member

- Need to acknowledge an improvement in performance
- Realize that managing performance is an essential part of your role as a manager
- Want to reassure a team member who's trying out a new skill
- Value the positive impact of feedback on your team
- Expect people to progress
- Believe in telling people how they're doing so they know where they stand
- Want to be respected as a manager
- Want to highlight the link between good individual performance and that of the organization

Once you identify reasons why giving clear and actionable feedback to your colleagues is important to you, you'll be able to give feedback that's sincere. What's more, as you try out the techniques in this book, reminding yourself of your reasons will help you keep applying your new skills.

EXERCISE

Think of a colleague who merits your praise and the gift of some positive feedback.

What are your reasons for wanting to give them feedback?

....

....

....

6. **BREVITY**
WAFFLE BE GONE

Now it's time to figure out what you will actually say to start the feedback conversation. Remember that good feedback is considered, clear and actionable – so this is where you put some time into figuring out what to say. With practice, you will find it easier to formulate your opening words.

A trap for beginners is waffling, whether out of anxiety and awkwardness, or due to feeling the need to elaborate a bit (or a lot) in order to justify having the conversation. This doesn't help anyone, as it just confuses things. Giving people an **EDGE** requires us to be brief, clear and to the point. Compare these two examples:

> "I just wanted to catch up with you for a few minutes to say I thought you did a great job in that presentation the other day. I know I'm not always the first person to say that someone's done a great job, but I thought I really ought to give you a pat on the back, as I was really pleased with it. Well done and keep up the good work. Oh, and another thing while I've got your attention..."

> "Well done in that presentation; I noticed you listened carefully to the financial questions at the end and checked a key point with the questioner before answering. I thought that showed respect and you got them nodding along. How do you think it went?"

Which example focused on the recipient? If you're in any doubt, count the frequency of "I" versus "you". Which example is clear about what the recipient did right? Which example would you prefer to receive? The first example is not the worst I've heard by far, but fails the criterion of being considered (it's a bit of a ramble), clear (what action merited the praise? The recipient won't have a clue) and actionable (what should the recipient do more of as a result? No idea).

The recipient of the first example will know the boss is pleased, but that's about it. The second example meets the criteria of being considered, clear and actionable; it gets to the point and then hands the mic to the recipient.

EXERCISE

How will you start the conversation? Script your opening lines and when you have, use a stopwatch to time how long it takes you to say them. Aim to be no longer than the second example above.

....

....

....

....

....

....

....

....

7. **HEALTHY EATING**
DON'T FEED
CLEVER PEOPLE
STUPID SANDWICHES

The question of sandwiches inevitably rears its head when the subject of feedback is under discussion. I'm sure you know very well which sandwiches I mean: let's refer to them as "feedback sandwiches" – although we both know they're called something rather less appetizing.

In case you've been spared this little snack, the idea with a "feedback sandwich" is that at first the recipient is told about something good they've done (a layer of buttered-up bread), then they're told something bad – i.e., that needs to get better – sandwiched in the middle (unpleasant filling), then they get another layer of good stuff (more buttered-up bread) at the end. The hapless recipient is thus expected to gratefully eat the sandwich handed to them. For example:

"I can see you've been working really hard on this project and – believe me – I really appreciate that. (There's the first layer of bread) *Now then, there's something I need you to sort out: your chaotic time-keeping. It's shambolic and you're all over the place. We can't have that, it looks really amateurish. You need to pull your socks up!* (That'll be the filling) *I'm sure you'll do the right thing, you usually do."* (There's the other layer of bread). Sandwich served. No response requested or required.

"What's so terrible about that?" I hear sandwich lovers cry. To which I answer that "feedback sandwiches" are:

- Confusing, as they drop mixed messages on the recipient.
- Good + bad + good = confused.
- Often ineffective, as the recipient tends to pay attention to either the bread or the filling, but not both. Our evolutionary wiring kicks in once again.
- A surefire way to devalue any genuine praise you want to give, as your recipient will soon learn to wait for the unpleasant news that inevitably follows.
- A monologue, as opposed to the dialogue that features when feedback is done well. No response is required from the recipient other than consuming the sandwich.
- Outmoded, as people increasingly expect feedback to be a democratic two-way process of giving and getting feedback,

whereas "feedback sandwiches" hark back to a more "command-and-control" approach.
- Insulting to recipients' intelligence – they're too smart to eat stupid sandwiches.

It would be far better and more effective to give people specific feedback that focuses on one aspect of their performance, keeping the balance in favour of praise.

EXERCISE
Recall "feedback sandwiches" you have received at work. Notice which elements you can remember. How have these experiences influenced your views on giving and receiving feedback?

....

....

....

....

....

....

....

8. WHEN
WHEN'S THE RIGHT TIME?

Participants in training workshops often ask "When is the right time for feedback?" The short answer is as soon as possible.

Keeping people in suspense until their next appraisal won't work for either of you. Chances are, you'll have forgotten the specific instances of praiseworthy performance when the next appraisal comes round. Your recipient may also have forgotten – in which case, you'll both have missed a great opportunity.

People increasingly want to know how they're doing and in real time, rather than being kept in suspense until the annual appraisal.

So when exactly is a good time? Take advantage of everyday situations that provide opportunities to give positive feedback, for example:

1. Before a meeting: *"You wrote the meeting notes promptly and clearly last time, so would you please do that again?"*

2. At the beginning of a project, at the kick-off meeting: *"You communicated with all the key stakeholders clearly and frequently on project Z. It helped keep us on track. How will you do that on this project?"*

3. Over a coffee, one-to-one: *"I've noticed you've been teaching Harry how to analyse data sets. He seems to be getting the hang of it. How's it going?"*

4. Briefing someone on a task: *"You explained the process really clearly at the site visit and the team got on with the job. How can you apply that to this project?"*

5. After a meeting or presentation: *"You spoke clearly and fluently in that presentation. I noticed you had the audience's attention. How do you think it went?"*

6. Stepping out to grab some lunch together: *"I want to thank you for covering for me when I was off last week. Everything seems to have gone really well. I'm keen to hear your views – can you tell me more?"*

7. After a conference call: *"I noticed that you asked really thorough questions about the scope on the call. What do you find works well with this supplier?"*

8. When reviewing someone's work with them: *"I think you've made a strong case for our suggestion. How would you like to take it from here?"*

9. At the end of a project, at the wrap-up meeting: *"Well done for getting the product launch done on time and on budget. What can we learn from this for future launches?"*

10. Before leaving work at the end of the day: *"Thanks for getting those figures in on time. It makes all our lives easier."*

That's ten situations to start you off; I'm sure you'll be able to think of more very quickly.

EXERCISE
Identify a colleague who merits praise for something well done.
When will you give them this positive feedback?

....

....

....

....

9. WHERE
PUBLIC OR PRIVATE?
PROS AND CONS

How do you like to be given positive feedback? Do you glow with pride and pleasure when you're praised publicly, say at a team meeting or at an all-staff gathering? Or would that situation have you running for cover? People are different and prefer to receive praise in different ways.

Some want their recognition to be loud, proud and very public (preferably with cheering, or at least applause). Others cherish the recognition far more when it's given privately, in a one-to-one conversation. There are pros and cons to each.

Praise given publicly communicates recognition for the recipient very powerfully. It also sends a signal to everyone present that the recognized action (and the impact it's had) is valued: "Do this and look what could happen to you". Team meetings, "town halls" where everyone shows up, "employee of the week, month or year" awards and office parties are typical opportunities for public praise. A potential downside is if people perceive any favouritism or unfairness, for example, if the same person, team or department is singled out all the time, or if a lack of opportunity may impede people's chances of getting public recognition.

Praise given privately can build trust and strong bonds between team members and their manager. Scheduled one-to-one catch-ups, regular coaching conversations and more spontaneous, informal opportunities are ideal for praising in private. A possible drawback is if the recipient doubts that the good news will be spread wider, for example in management discussions about candidates for promotion and rewards.

Why not do both? You could set up a one-to-one positive feedback conversation first and at the end of it ask your recipient if they'd be happy for you to mention what they've done well at the next team meeting. Explain that you want to share examples of people doing the job right, so that everyone knows who to watch and learn what good performance looks like.

EXERCISE

First, recall times when you've received praise in public.
How did you feel receiving praise in public? Contrast this with
when you've received praise in private, one-to-one with someone. What was different and which worked best for you?

....

....

....

....

....

Next, thinking of the colleagues you'll be praising in the very
near future, what do you know about their preferences that will
guide you about the best place to give them feedback?

....

....

....

....

....

10. GET THE HABIT
GIVING POSITIVE STROKES

Now's the time to start giving positive feedback to people, based on what you've observed them doing well and the impact it's having.

Identify three people to whom you'll give positive feedback within the next 24 hours. They can be colleagues, people in your professional network or friends.

Name

....

What have you observed this person doing well?

....

....

What impact has the action had?

....

....

How will you start the conversation?

....

....

What question will you ask to give them the mic?

....

....

....

Name

....

What have you observed this person doing well?

....

....

What impact has the action had?

....

....

How will you start the conversation?

....

....

What question will you ask to give them the mic?

....

....

....

Name

....

What have you observed this person doing well?

....

....

What impact has the action had?

....

....

How will you start the conversation?

....

....

What question will you ask to give them the mic?

....

....

....

PART THREE

COURSE
CORRECTION

A WORD ON COURSE CORRECTION

At some point, you will need to give someone feedback to help correct their course of action. Many managers shirk this responsibility, not wanting to have a "difficult conversation".

But what happens if no one on the team is getting feedback for improvement? Doing nothing at all sends its own powerful signal: "Poor or substandard performance is tolerated around here" and "you can get away with it – everyone else does".

Or what happens if only one or two people attract the negative feedback, while others are seen to get away with it? The atmosphere can get resentful, toxic and affect the business.

If you manage a team of people, managing their performance is an essential part of your role, and that includes correcting their course when performance needs to improve. Corrective feedback can transform someone's performance.

Welcome to your job.

1. **FAIRNESS**
TREAD CAREFULLY

First, some words of warning. Take criticism too far and you could end up alienating a colleague or worse, find yourself in hot water, accused of harassing a fellow employee. Or if you are constantly singling out one individual for extreme course correction, it may be perceived by them (and their colleagues) as unfair treatment.

However, if you're a manager, the buck stops with you when it comes to nipping any poor performance in the bud before it becomes a bigger problem. To err is human: it's inevitable that at some point you will need to give someone feedback on their performance with the aim of helping them identify the steps they'll take to improve.

Remember how we're wired: we often default to fault-finding mode at work, added to which we all have biases we're largely unaware of. You may unintentionally be cutting more slack for someone who operates in a similar style to you than someone else who's doing the same job to the same standard, but in a different way.

Or your "fight-or-flight" response may be kicking in as you see that someone is struggling to deliver, but their stressed-out demeanour has put you off having a conversation with them about their performance. You're worried they'll get upset or angry, so you keep putting it off – and your "flight" response wins. These conversations can be tricky to navigate if you're unprepared, and the recipient's response may be hard to predict. Given the potential risks, it's no wonder that plenty of managers duck out of giving feedback for improvement.

Two keys to unlocking this impasse are: getting the ongoing balance of praise to correction right (at least 3:1) and giving feedback little and often.

Don't put it off; people need to know you've noticed substandard performance and that you expect it to improve.

EXERCISE

Think of a team member and note three things they do well that merit praise and one aspect of their performance that needs to improve. If you find you come up with several improvement areas, rank them in order of impact on the organization and take the first one.
Repeat for all team members.

....

....

....

2. ASSESSMENT
WHAT NEEDS
TO CHANGE?

Now that you've identified the priority areas for improvement, it's time to get crystal clear on why the person needs to change their behaviour. You need evidence, not opinion, so start with the results. For example:

- Was a client angry at receiving a document because it was strewn with typos and grammatical errors?
- Were penalties incurred because costs were allowed to run out of control before the rest of the team were alerted?
- Did a known technical risk go untested, resulting in a delivery failure?
- Was a key component late going to a supplier, resulting in late delivery?
- Did an important presentation go badly due to lack of preparation?

Get clear on what actually happened – its impact on the individual, colleagues and others – and the overall results of the action. There may have been a complaint or a financial penalty to pay, or others had to pitch in to get the job back on track, causing extra workload. Was a contract lost, or reputational damage done to the firm? This is no time for drama; it's time to establish exactly what led to an unwanted end result.

What actions were involved? What did the individual do – or not do? Beware lapsing into adjectives here: "defensive", "domineering", "immature" etc., can only make matters worse, as they're critical and judgmental.

At this point, you may have clarified where the wrong course was taken and its subsequent impact. If so, you're ready to move on to the next stage. Or, you may have realized that the perceived short-coming has had hardly any adverse impact. It's just something that bugs you, one of your pet peeves. Well done, you've probably just spotted a bias at work. In which case, you can simply let people get on with what they've been doing, so long as the desired results aren't compromised and coworkers aren't adversely affected.

EXERCISE
Refer back to the improvement areas in the previous exercise.
Chart the course backwards from the end result, which was the reason why a change is needed. Next, note the impact on others and what actually happened. Finally, focus on the exact behaviour that led to it.

What is the action that needs to addressed?

Action?	What happened?	Impact?	Results?
....	....	....	....
....	....	....	....
....	....	....	....

3. **SENSITIVITY**
WALK IN
THEIR SHOES

If you've just plotted out the course of poor performance in the previous exercise, accept that remembering screw-ups isn't going to make you happy, but at the same time, getting angry won't help either. Being in the "fight" zone of the stress response isn't the best state in which to deliver the gift of feedback that will benefit the recipient. You'll need a cool head and a warm heart. We have to keep the recipient in mind – what's in it for them if they get this feedback? What's likely to happen if they don't get this feedback?

Remember that you won't be the only one dealing with the fight-or-flight response in what can be a tricky situation for both of you. Your recipient may well find the conversation stressful. Research suggests our physiological response to critical feedback is very similar to when we experience physical pain. Ouch.

If corrective feedback can be painful, then why should we still do it? Because the alternative could be even more painful. When you give people feedback that's balanced in favour of praise and people get used to that, they'll be more likely to trust that you have their interests at heart when you give corrective feedback. Remember, corrective needn't be a negative experience – someone's performance can dramatically improve as a result.

Many managers are unsure how feedback recipients will respond, and they allow that uncertainty to put them off having feedback conversations. The simple way to get through this obstacle is to consider the recipient's likely response by looking at the situation from their perspective, as though you're walking in their shoes. Your ability to do this will vary according to how well you know the individual and how accurately you've observed their responses in the past, but it's never too late to start practising.

It's important to note the value of anticipating how the recipient might perceive the corrective feedback. If this is seen to be unfair, for example, if they believe they're constantly being singled out due to bias, or others are taking an identical wrong course yet getting away with it, they can suffer the same unhealthy hormonal cocktail as someone under extreme stress.[5]

EXERCISE

Picture your prospective feedback recipient sitting opposite you. It may help to close your eyes, if it's safe for you to do so. What does this person:

- Respond well to?

  ....

- Respond badly to?

  ....

- Value about the work they do?

  ....

- Give top priority to?

  ....

- Do when they're under pressure?

  ....

If you start a conversation with them with the words, *"I want to give you some feedback,"* how might they react?

....

....

4. PREPARATION
HOW WILL YOU START THE CONVERSATION?

When you're giving someone feedback for improvement, the first few seconds, those first few words, are absolutely crucial. That's why it's essential to prepare for this in advance: you want to be focused on the recipient and their responses, not ensnared by your own thoughts and feelings.

I recommend writing down what you want to say for both the "**E**xplain the action" and "**D**escribe the impact" stages of the **EDGE** feedback framework. Use your notes to rehearse, refine and edit what you'll say. Giving people an **EDGE** works for both giving praise and feedback for improvement or course correction, as the principles are the same. You're giving considered, clear and actionable feedback on someone's behaviour as part of a two-way conversation. Use these "how to" and "how not to" examples to prompt your thinking about how you'll start the conversation.

How to

"I noticed you read off your slides in the presentation. The audience ended up looking at the handouts more than they looked at you and didn't ask any questions."

"I saw you using your smartphone throughout the team meeting and you didn't contribute much to the discussion."

"I need to give you some feedback about that meeting, as I heard you interrupt the client whenever she spoke."

"I saw you weren't taking any notes in the project update meeting, although after the last update you offered to get all the agreed actions typed up and distributed the same day."

How not to

"I thought your presentation was unprofessional."

"Just what were you finding so utterly fascinating on your phone that was more deserving of your miniscule attention span than our team meeting?"

"You were rather aggressive and abrupt with Sophie when she asked you a perfectly reasonable question."

"Honestly, you are so sloppy about following up on meetings. I give up! Why do you keep asking me what happened? Were you just there in body but not mind, is that it?"

EXERCISE

First, write down the action that's prompted the feedback.

....

....

Next, consider the impact that it's had, sticking to the facts. It's essential to note how you know.

....

....

Remember you need evidence to back up your feedback, so ask yourself if an impartial observer would verify what you're about to say. Snap judgments have no place here. You're a credible witness – not the judge and jury. Your factual statement for starting the conversation needs to be brief, yet sufficiently clear.

....

....

....

....

....

5. **DISCUSSION**
DEVELOP THE DIALOGUE

If you're going to give someone an **EDGE**, you need to get to the stage of **G**iving them the mic pretty quickly. This is vital when the feedback concerns an action that needs to improve, or else your recipient could feel cornered. The sooner you hand over the mic, the sooner your recipient can articulate why this has happened and you can have a conversation.

Hog the mic and your feedback could turn into a rant. You may have felt some justifiable anger at whatever transgression you witnessed, but relaying that anger to the recipient won't help either of you. If you're angry, it's worth taking a moment (or five) to get calm and completely clear.

Giving your recipient the mic means inviting them into a conversation, and the best way to do that is to ask them a question. Keep it short and simple, such as:

"How do you think it went?"
"What impact do you think that has?"
"How do you think X felt about that?"
"What are your thoughts on that?"
"How do you feel about that?"

Top tip: avoid using "why" at this point in the conversation. For example "why did you do that?" If the topic of conversation were your own shortcomings, how would you feel on the receiving end of "why"? Many of us may perceive being asked "why" as an aggressive challenge and go on the defensive. Or a "why" may end up as a whine, like a child demanding to know why they can't have more ice cream, which won't help matters at all. You may of course need to establish "why" your recipient acted as they did, but other forms of questioning will get you there more amicably.

The next part can be testing for any feedback giver: shut up and listen. Listen very carefully to what your recipient has to say – and be prepared for them to need a little time to say it. Much of our behaviour is automatic, so your recipient may genuinely have no idea they were doing what you've just pointed out to them. Pay very close attention to what is said and how it is said. Don't "reload" while they are speaking – as in rehearsing your next statement and therefore not listening while they speak. Focus on their words, their voice and their expression – all of which are valuable feedback on how they feel right now. Stay open to this and you will be able to make progress.

EXERCISE
Brainstorm a handy selection of questions that will enable you to give the mic to the recipient of your feedback.
How will you invite them to join the conversation?

....

....

6. **HONESTY**
DON'T
DRESS IT UP

At this point, you may be feeling slightly uncomfortable, wondering if this **EDGE** approach isn't just a touch too... blunt.

If you're finding this approach too direct, beware of the temptation to dress up the feedback by adding frills and embellishments in an attempt to make it more palatable for your recipient. Maybe you're struggling to edit your feedback for improvement down to just a few short sentences. If so, you may be looking at something like this:

> *"I know you've been working really hard lately, and I do really value your contribution but... and I can see you're under a lot of pressure but there's just this small thing... anyway, I just wanted to comment on what happened back there in that meeting. You know, the part where you were getting questions from the client and you were rather pushy. I appreciate that some of the questions were tough but ... could you just have a think about that?"*

Feedback like this isn't helpful because:

- Sandwich alert: there's an element of "buttering up" the recipient (especially when uttered in an almost apologetic tone) before landing the comments about what needs to improve.
- What prompted the feedback hasn't been clearly identified – we don't know what the recipient did (and neither will they).
- "Pushy" is the speaker's subjective opinion of the recipient's behaviour. The recipient and indeed others at the meeting may not agree.
- The impact is unclear – there's no cause and effect.
- Too much verbiage before the mic is handed over – this is unlikely to engage the recipient in conversation.

We all need to know how we're doing – even if the feedback can sometimes be hard to hear. If you're finding this approach too direct, please pause to consider if this is due to your own discomfort about giving (and receiving) feedback in the past. Remember: it's not about you. Instead, try focusing on the benefit to your recipient when you give honest, clear and actionable feedback that's intended to help them correct their course.

EXERCISE

Look back at your draft feedback from the previous two exercises and remove any bows, ribbons and embellishments.

....

7. **ADAPTABILITY**
DIFFERENT
RESPONSES

Once your feedback recipient is given the mic, then what? Anything can happen. You'll need to be ready to adapt according to how they respond. For example, they may:

- Have been blissfully unaware of the action that prompted the feedback and need a moment to take it in.
- Be painfully aware that they have been falling short in some way, but weren't quite sure where they were going wrong.
- Know all too well that they need to correct course, but aren't quite sure what to do instead.
- Be relieved that you've initiated this conversation, as they want to improve, but were hesitant about asking you.
- Get upset and take this instance of a needed improvement as an example of how they're just "completely rubbish at everything".
- React angrily, as they're stressed, and your feedback is the final straw.
- Dispute your version of events and respond with a tirade about all the times you've been less than perfect.

Your recipient may have one or a combination of these responses, or they may even respond in another way altogether. They'll most likely accept that course correction is needed and the conversation can progress. You can simply ask them a coaching question such as, *"What will you do differently next time?"* or *"How can you handle that in future?"* – and let them respond.

But what if their reaction is difficult? How can you adapt and ensure it's a productive discussion? If you've clearly identified the behaviour in question, there will be little room for manoeuvre. If you've been giving them plenty of praise up to this point, your recipient could feel jolted out of that warm glow they've been experiencing, but as long as you maintain a balance over time, they'll know where they stand with you.

You've got some options:
- Explain that you're giving them feedback to help them improve and step up – not to put them down.
- Calmly repeat what you noticed – the action and its impact.
- Ask them what impact they noticed at the time.
- Explain that you care about their performance and that you will give them the support they need.
- Offer them time to collect their thoughts and calm down.

EXERCISE
Think back to how your colleagues have responded to feedback before – whether the feedback was focused on praise or course correction. Consider how self-aware they are. If they were to react badly to feedback, how would you adapt?

....

8. ENCOURAGEMENT
ENDING WELL

Let's say that you've given someone considered, clear and actionable feedback about what needs to improve, invited them to join the conversation and they've responded. Even if the recipient needed to walk away and calm down, the conversation was resumed, as you both want to resolve the issue. By this point you will have covered the **E**, **D** and **G** in **EDGE**. Now you need to **E**nd the conversation in a way that encourages the recipient to commit to taking different actions.

Often your recipient will identify what they'll change and do differently in the future. Sometimes they may not always get there at first; if that happens, you'll need to offer further coaching questions to help them clarify the next steps.

"What's a small step you can take to get started?"
"Who can you think of who's good at that? How do they go about it?"
"What will make the most difference?"
"When will you have an opportunity to try it out?"
"How will you know you're progressing?"

It's a good idea to allow feedback recipients to articulate the new behaviour for themselves. We are more likely to take responsibility for what we say we're going to do than for what someone else tells us to do. Ensure there's commitment to act. Once they've done that, all that's needed from you is a nod and a smile.

What if your recipient can't come up with their own suggestions for course correction? You will need to offer two or three suggestions of different actions they can try instead of what they've been doing. Coach them to identify when and how they can practise.

If the improvement you seek is more complex than a simple behaviour change, such as developing a new skill, you need to be ready to provide support for your feedback recipient or help them get it. However, the responsibility for development should remain with them.

"What support do you need from me?"
"How do you want to develop your skills at this?"
"When's the next training course on this going to run?"
"Who would be a good coach for you in this area?"
"What else do you need from me to do a great job?"

End on a positive note by giving them the last word.

EXERCISE

What will you say to ensure the conversation ends well, with the recipient's commitment?

....

....

....

....

....

....

....

....

9. CONSISTENCY
SHOW YOU'VE NOTICED

Phew. You did it. You started a conversation with a colleague about an aspect of their performance that needed to improve. Air got cleared. All went well. So now what?

Now you need to model consistency. You and this individual discussed what needed to improve, and when it does, you need to show that you've noticed. You'll need to keep your powers of observation sharp, to spot your feedback recipient getting it right. Are they trying to do things differently? What behaviour have they changed? What progress are they making? No matter how small the shift, if you spot a change in the right direction, give positive feedback each time you notice.

"You gave the client your full attention and she gave us a really comprehensive brief. Good work."
"Well done, I noticed you taking notes and checking facts in that meeting."
"You delivered that presentation well, focusing on the audience and getting their input. I thought it was a success, what do you think?"

If a new skill is required in order to improve, remember that learners take longer – mastering a skill takes practice. Provide opportunity and recognize effort; positive feedback from you will give the learner a sense of progress.

What if you're paying close attention to this colleague's behaviour and can't see any change for the better? You might need to dig a bit deeper to unearth the cause. What could they gain from staying the same? Staying stuck can happen for a number of reasons: fear of failure, memory of past attempts that didn't work well, anxiety, lack of motivation, or even fear of succeeding. Have a conversation with them about the obstacles they perceive to be in their path to improved performance. They may need support and coaching from you or a subject matter expert.

If all the right conditions are in place and you still don't see an improvement, it could be worth checking with one or two trusted colleagues to see if they've noticed any change. Maybe your biases are messing with your powers of observation. Or it might just be that you are part of the problem, and now it's your turn to get some feedback – more on this later.

Ultimately, if performance doesn't change for the better, the feedback must be repeated; first, to show you've noticed that the improvement you discussed hasn't yet happened and second, to emphasize that change is expected.

EXERCISE
When people make a change and learn new skills, they often need support. When you have consciously worked to improve your own performance, who and what have helped you?

....

10. GET THE HABIT
STEERING FOR
COURSE CORRECTION

If you've been developing the feedback habit from Part 2, you'll have banked plenty of praise (and if you haven't, I suggest you get that habit before you even think of starting on course correction).

As you begin to give feedback for improvement, you must continue to keep praising consistently whenever you observe something good. Remember, this is about giving feedback, not veering from praise to course correction depending on how you feel today.

Identify three people and what each person is doing that requires course corrective feedback. They can be colleagues, people in your professional network or friends.

Who have you noticed who could improve with a small course correction?

....

....

What is it they're doing?

....

....

What impact does that action have?

....

....

Why should this behaviour change?

....

....

When will you have the conversation and give them the gift of feedback?

....

....

Who have you noticed who could improve with a small course correction?

....

....

What is it they're doing?

....

....

What impact does that action have?

....

....

Why should this behaviour change?

....

....

When will you have the conversation and give them the gift of feedback?

....

....

Who have you noticed who could improve with a small course correction?

....

....

What is it they're doing?

....

....

What impact does that action have?

....

....

Why should this behaviour change?

....

....

When will you have the conversation and give them the gift of feedback?

....

....

PART FOUR

UPWARDS

AND

OUTWARDS

A WORD ABOUT GIVING FEEDBACK UPWARDS AND OUTWARDS

Once you start getting the feedback habit, you'll soon spot heaps of opportunities to give feedback to people you encounter as you go about your work. These people may be higher up in the organization ('upwards'), or your employers' clients, suppliers or other key stakeholders ('outwards'), so you'll need to moderate your feedback approach carefully.

Why? Unlike your team, these people probably work with you less frequently and it's highly unlikely that their performance is your responsibility. The boundaries are very different. Organizational culture comes into play, as does the distribution of power in hierarchies. There are risks as well as rewards when you give feedback within significant professional relationships. That's why I suggest you only start giving feedback upwards and outwards once you've mastered the art with your immediate colleagues. That way you'll be more likely to get the right response – and results.

1. DIRECTION
WHO NEEDS TO KNOW – AND WHY?

Who needs to know? Here are some examples of people who could benefit from being given your gift of feedback:

- Your boss
- Your boss's boss
- Project team members
- Fellow participants on a training course
- Peers
- Hotel staff at a conference
- Customers
- External consultants
- Service users
- Professional associations
- Former colleagues
- So-called support functions: IT, HR, finance, office management
- Contacts in your professional network
- Recruitment consultants
- Regulatory or compliance bodies
- Contractors
- Suppliers

- Clients
- Job applicants
- New joiners

So, why would you want to give feedback upwards and outwards to these people? Feedback usually becomes necessary because of a positive or negative impact on working relationships or performance – or both. You may have noticed something that is worthy of comment, good or bad. Some such situations are listed below:

- Your boss sends emails to you and your team very late at night.
- The staff at the venue for your recent conference stayed late working with you to check that everything was set up as requested.
- A client has kept one of your team waiting in their reception area for an hour.
- Someone in the IT department has been providing one-to-one coaching support to one of your team.
- A job applicant turned up for their first interview evidently unprepared and unaware of what your company does.
- Your boss lavishes praise on more outgoing members of the team, whereas quieter people seem to be overlooked.
- Your professional association's website keeps crashing every time you are just about to hit "send" on its "please submit your feedback on our site" survey.
- Two digital specialists – not your department – have been working all weekend on a project for your client.
- The name of a recruitment consultant who specializes in your sector seems to have cropped up on your immediate team members' social media profiles a fair bit lately. You're concerned she's about to try to find them jobs elsewhere.

Before you launch into giving feedback upwards and outwards, one question is worth a pause for thought: are you the best person to give this feedback? If it's a simple issue for your immediate boss, you probably are. But bear in mind that upwards and outwards working relationships are more complex, and an indirect approach may be more diplomatic – and more effective.

For example, you might want to have a word with HR about the best way to handle the recruitment consultant. Your professional association might take a complaint about their website more seriously if a senior colleague were to get in touch. It depends on the characters involved and what's at stake.

EXERCISE

Why and to whom do you need to give upwards and outwards feedback? What's impacting your immediate team, within or beyond the organization, which you think is worthy of comment?

....

....

Who are the people that need to receive your feedback?

....

Are you the best person to give this feedback? If not, who is?

....

2. CULTURE
"HOW WE DO THINGS ROUND HERE"

When feedback is a gift that's genuinely useful to the recipient, they'll want to hear it, right? Not necessarily, unfortunately. Some organizational cultures are very hierarchical, command-and-control places; some clients consider themselves immune from feedback of any kind; some contractors immediately go on the defensive while others might not pass on the praise, and a few people simply seem unable to handle feedback whether it's positive or corrective.

Culture in organizations is best described by the phrase "How we do things around here". You know, the unspoken stuff that always seems to trip up new joiners? That's it. When you hear "that's not how we do it here" or "that's not how we operate" or "what we're about", that's the firm's culture showing up. If you're giving feedback to people in organizations – yours or other people's – be very sensitive to the prevailing culture. Try to identify:

- How are things done "around here"?
- What are the organization's stated values? How are they related to the behaviour that's prompting you to give feedback?
- How hierarchical is the organization?
- What is the prevailing attitude toward plain speaking and transparency?
- How formal or informal is the working atmosphere?
- How new is your prospective feedback recipient to your organization – or to working with you?

Top tip: as you get to know different external contacts, such as suppliers or clients, create your own pen portraits of their culture using these questions. Revisit and update your pen portraits from time to time.

Observe how the organization's culture shows up before you take action and, if in doubt, ask for advice about how to approach it. For example, how might:

- Your boss respond to praise from you?
- A supplier react to feedback about them letting your team down?
- A senior manager feel about you giving them corrective feedback?
- A contractor feel about positive feedback on a rush job they delivered?
- An external consultant respond to your corrective feedback on how they handled questions from your client in a recent meeting?

EXERCISE

Refer back to the person or people you identified in the previous exercise.

What's the cultural context? What is typical behaviour in the organization?

....

....

Consider how this person generally responds.

Do they get uncomfortable with positive feedback and brush it off?

....

Do they rebut any feedback that even hints at shortcomings on their part?

....

What generally works well with them – and what doesn't?

....

Whose opinions do they respect – and why?

....

....

3. EVALUATION
WHAT ARE THE RISKS IF YOU DO (OR DON'T) GIVE FEEDBACK?

Before you take that step upwards or outwards, you need to weigh up the risks and rewards.

Risks if you DON'T give feedback	Risks if you DO give feedback
· Your peers may believe you don't notice the effort that others, for example, their direct reports, are making.	· You may – inadvertently – start a turf war with another manager.
· Your boss may have no idea of the impact of their actions – for good or otherwise – on you and your colleagues.	· You might upset a customer if the feedback is negative.
· Cries of "it's not fair!" may be heard from your team about the unhelpful behaviour of another team if it's silently tolerated.	· If you haven't done your homework, you may blow a one-off lapse out of proportion.
· Working relationships can be damaged over time.	· Working relationships might be damaged if you give feedback to someone who is particularly sensitive.
· The atmosphere can get resentful or worse, toxic and nasty.	· You may surprise or even shock someone simply by the very act of giving feedback, for example, to your boss.
· Whatever the problem has been, it will get bigger.	
· If you finally do raise a problem, you'll no doubt be met with, "Why didn't you say so before?"	

Rewards if you DON'T give feedback	**Rewards if you DO give feedback**
· You might buy some much-needed time – handy if you need to get your facts straight. · You could have a quiet life – well, for now at least.	· You could nip a problem in the bud. · Working relationships may improve if you give feedback and invite some in return. · You could flag a problem the recipient was unaware of. · Better results may follow feedback, whether positive or negative. · You might bank some brownie points. · Your team will know you've got their back if the feedback is in their defence. · The recipient may benefit from feedback that simply shows you've noticed.

EXERCISE

Time to weigh it up.

What are the risks if you DON'T give any feedback?

....

....

....

What are the rewards if you DON'T give any feedback?

....

....

....

What are the risks if you DO give feedback?

....

....

What are the rewards if you DO give feedback?

....

....

4. **PLANNING** MARSHALL YOUR EVIDENCE

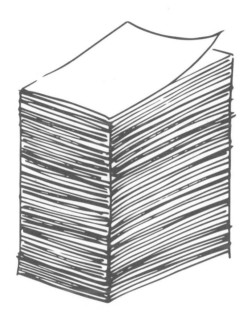

Let's say you've weighed up the risks and rewards and decided that it's still well worth giving your feedback to someone beyond your immediate team. The **EDGE** framework still applies, so you will need to get crystal clear on what has prompted your feedback; both the action and its impact. Whether you're giving high praise or reasons why improvement is essential, you need evidence. Remember, you're venturing beyond the boundaries of your immediate team here, and some might say beyond your pay grade. You may inadvertently fall foul of a multitude of an organization's unwritten rules. So there must be no wriggle room about what you're going to say has happened and the impact it's had.

Consider times, places and the people involved. Who else might have observed or experienced the behaviour in question? You may need to check in with others to get your facts straight, and don't be afraid to push for clear examples of actions if the adjectives start flying. How did the person "get aggressive" on the phone? What did they do? What did they say?

Negative feedback example:

A delivery from your stationery supplier arrived a day late. When you called to find out where it was, you were told the van had broken down and delivery would be made the next day. As a result, two of the office management staff had to go to a high-street shop and buy paper at a higher price, which they then had to bring back in a taxi.

Positive feedback example:
Your printer's sales rep invited two junior members of your team for a site visit so they could see a project progress from computer file through to finished article. They returned enthused and much better able to explain to clients what's involved and how long certain processes can take.

If you're going to give feedback on behalf of your team, for example if they've experienced bad behaviour from a contractor, ensure you collect multiple examples from as many team members as possible.

Then notice what consistently crops up in the different accounts. The same principle applies if your team is nominating a contractor for hero status.

When you've nailed the actions, then you can move on to the impact that they've had, for which you'll also need detailed examples in order to have a productive conversation.

EXERCISE

What evidence do you have of the action that merits feedback?

....

....

....

....

What's the evidence for the impact this behaviour has had?

....

....

....

....

5. **PERMISSION**
GET OFF TO A
GOOD START

When you're giving feedback to someone you don't work with every day or who is more senior or much more experienced than you, you'll need to take extra care to get the conversation off to a good start. Those you deal with less often will need to be gently primed so that the feedback is received in the spirit intended – as a gift that will benefit them. Whether the feedback you are about to give is seeking improvement or showing appreciation, you will need to ask permission to open the dialogue.

"Can I give you some feedback about what just happened on that call?"
"Is it OK to give you some feedback? Is now a good time?"
"I want to give you some feedback about your conference speech."
"I need to give you some feedback – when's a good time?"
"There's some feedback from my team that I would like to discuss with you."

Don't waffle on here, get to the point and get permission to continue. You may be met with a slightly stunned "er, OK" or "Really? Do I need to sit down for this?" Pay attention to your body language – and that of your recipient, who will also be interpreting these signs – your facial expression, eye contact, gestures and tone of voice will speak volumes.

EXERCISE

How will you seek permission to give feedback, in just a few words?

....

....

Record into your smartphone how you will ask permission.
Now play it back and imagine you're the recipient. What would you think?

....

....

How would you feel?

....

....

....

Once you've got permission to proceed, you can move on to **E**xplaining the action and **D**escribing the impact it has had, adding a question so you can **G**ive them the mic.

For example:

"I appreciated your honesty in your conference speech. When you explained how the company's been performing, it all made sense. I now know what to say to my team. Do you have any tips for sharing the main message?"

"My team members have been getting emails from you at all hours of the night and it's causing so much stress that I need to raise this with you. Can we work out a better way for you to communicate with them?"

EXERCISE

Script what you will say to **E**xplain the action, **D**escribe the impact and **G**ive the mic to your feedback recipient. Record this into your smartphone. Now play it back and imagine you're the recipient. What would you think?

....

How would you feel?

....

....

6. **SENSIBILITY**
STICK OR TWIST

What if your feedback doesn't land very well and the recipient responds badly once they've got the mic? You can stick with the conversation and do your best to keep it on track. Or you might twist and hit the pause button. What can you do if your feedback recipient:

Tells you it's none of your business?

Remind them of the impact on time, cost, quality, your team's morale and performance – and that these things are both their and your business. Explain you're after a mutually beneficial result.

Gets upset?

Give them time to digest the feedback and ask a question or two to check that they understand and accept your account of what actually happened. Coach them on what they can and will do to rectify performance that needs to improve. Ask them to suggest what they'll do differently.

Reacts angrily?

If they really go off the deep end, say you'll continue the conversation when they're ready and have had time to digest the feedback. This reaction may of course be the exact behaviour that's prompted the feedback, in which case you'll need to stay reasonable and point out that this is what you mean (without being smug).

Challenges your feedback?

Ask a question to check their understanding of the situation. If you're dealing with someone who's known to dispute negative feedback, be sure to get corroboration and organize your evidence beforehand. Stay focused on the action in question and don't let the discussion stray beyond that.

Insists that you achieve the impossible?

Simply saying "it can't be done" isn't going to help. "If this then that" is a better tactic with an unreasonable boss or customer. Even the most belligerent client can understand cause and effect. So you'll need to explain that if everyone works overtime, then the costs will escalate; if the video has to be done all over again, then the deadline will have to shift; if the recruitment budget reduction means you can't hire more people, then freelancers and short-term contractors will have to be brought in. Be prepared to stand your ground here and haggle if necessary.

What if your recipient really isn't sure what's needed? That's next.

EXERCISE
Brainstorm your worst-case scenarios for giving upwards feedback to someone in a more senior position.
How will you handle the challenge?

....

....

....

....

....

....

....

....

....

7. **SUBSTITUTION**
SPELL IT OUT

There may be situations where you'll find that no amount of gentle coaching to elicit corrective action seems to get through.

I've found that upwards and outward relationships sometimes need a more direct approach to correct course. Whether it's suppliers who appear to repeat the same mistakes, or internal support departments that just don't seem to be listening, asking them to come up with their own solutions can be frustrating for both parties. Remember, with upwards and outward relationships, the boundaries are different and you're probably not the person directly responsible for performance, so you'll have to adapt to get the right result.

- Your busy CEO needs you to stop asking questions and start making suggestions.
- Your error-prone supplier needs you to suggest what they do instead, because as far as they're concerned it's no big deal.
- Your unresponsive support department has no idea how they're perceived within the organization, because nobody's ever told them (and they've never asked).

In those situations, you can take a more active role in the **G**ive them the mic stage of **EDGE**.

You'll start by **E**xplaining the action and **D**escribing its impact as normal:

"I need to raise something with you: when you turn up late for meetings with our biggest client, they complain while we wait for you."

"I want to give you some feedback on the last batch of flyers you delivered. They went to the wrong address and it took a while to trace and retrieve them."

"I need to give you some feedback: my team called your help desk two days ago and there's been no response. They're now held up on a project and risk delivering late."

Then when you ask a question to **G**ive them the mic, you structure it differently, giving one or two (no more) suggestions and asking for their reaction.

"How about we have the meetings earlier in the day so that you can start the day with them, or via conference call so you can join the call from wherever you are? Which do you think would work best?"

"What if your driver uses a scanner app on their phone and sends us the signed delivery note there and then, so we don't need to keep checking? Can you do that?"

"Instead of a phone line, how about online live chat, where one of your team acknowledges and says when they'll be here? How could you make that work?"

You can see that this approach is more prescriptive, suggesting what to do instead. It works well when dealing with "get-to-the-point" people and service providers. Please note, this approach should be used sparingly with those you manage, as they could easily see it as micromanaging.

8. **TOGETHERNESS**
FEEDBACK
WITHIN TEAMS

I've worked with some brilliant teams, and over time have noticed that one of their hallmarks is honesty with themselves and each other. They're focused on their goals, while being highly aware of their own and each team member's strengths and weaknesses.

The very best teams take that honesty to a higher level by frequently giving and receiving feedback, and by holding each other accountable. It's been my observation that weaker, less successful teams seem to find complete honesty and mutual accountability hard to achieve, and if they do give feedback, it can be clumsy and unclear. How does giving the gift of feedback work in teams? If feedback is provided:

Constantly – everyday events such as project kick-offs, management updates and wrap meetings are used as opportunities to give and get feedback, in order to improve. There's no waiting for the year-end or some special occasion; feedback is given informally in real time and (a little) more formally in meetings. Feedback is wired into what they do day-in, month-out.

Considerately – there is genuine respect for each other, which shows up as being mindful of the emotions involved. Feedback is given with great care, motivated by a desire to help and support each other. It won't surprise you to know that the feedback is weighted toward positive much more than negative.

Simply – when there are strong and open working relationships, there's no need to dress up feedback; it's delivered simply and clearly. When the whole team reviews their performance, for example at a wrap-up, I've found it can help to have a few simple questions to guide discussion, such as: "What worked well?" "What didn't work so well?" "What have we learned?" "What will we do differently next time?"

Equally – everyone contributes and gets given feedback regardless of seniority; no one is above it all. Everyone's opinion is equally valid.

Clearly – one team I know uses "stop, start and continue" to give each other feedback at their off-site sessions. Since they got the hang of ditching adjectives in favour of observable actions, this has proved highly effective. There have been smiles, as well as "Ooh, didn't know I'd been doing that." This only works if "equally" above is observed.

EXERCISE

Look at your calendar for the next few weeks and highlight at least three opportunities for feedback within work teams you're a member of.

....

....

....

....

....

....

....

....

....

....

9. **BALANCE**
NOW FOR THE GOOD NEWS

A great way to reinforce your positive feedback to the people you manage is to delegate the conversation upwards. It's also a smart way to manage upwards, which all too often can focus on relaying bad news. Involving your boss in good news strikes a better balance. It works like this: say that Jackie has recently been making a great effort to deliver work on time (since getting feedback from you that this wasn't happening often enough). Once you're seeing consistent improvement – enough to have already merited your praise – you can mention this to your manager.

"I thought you'd be pleased to hear that Jackie's making a great effort to get her work done on time. I've noticed a big improvement that has benefitted the rest of the team – less stress, unrest and more cooperation. I've told her this, and if you were to say something next time you see her, it would really give her a boost."

Giving feedback in this way has several advantages:

- Your boss has a "good news" job to do and is more than happy to do it.
- Jackie is going to be delighted that someone senior is remarking on her improved performance, which should help sustain it.
- Your team management skills will impress your manager without you having to blow your own trumpet.

This approach can also work well with your peers about their team members and with managers in other departments.

"I want to give you some feedback about Daniel's input on that recent tender. He delivered exactly what we wanted when we wanted it, but not only that, he came up with lots of suggestions about additional ways of making the most of the data. We were really impressed and included his ideas in the tender document."

You can also use the feedback approach externally, such as with the managers of your regular contacts at suppliers.

EXERCISE
Identify a manager to whom you can give some positive feedback about either one of your team, or a member of their team or department.

Who will you speak to?

....

....

....

....

What will you say?

....

....

....

....

....

....

....

10. GET THE HABIT
STEPPING UP

Identify three people to whom you're going to give some feedback.
They could be your manager, one of your peers, an external supplier
or client. Aim for more positive feedback than negative.

Name

....

What behaviour have you observed?

....

....

What impact has the behaviour had?

....

....

How will you start the conversation?

....

....

What question will you ask to give them the mic?

....

....

....

Name

....

What behaviour have you observed?

....

....

What impact has the behaviour had?

....

....

How will you start the conversation?

....

....

What question will you ask to give them the mic?

....

....

....

Name

....

What behaviour have you observed?

....

....

What impact has the behaviour had?

....

....

How will you start the conversation?

....

....

What question will you ask to give them the mic?

....

....

....

Note how your recipients respond.

Do they agree with the feedback?

What changes do you notice as a result of the feedback?

What if you can't identify three people at this stage in your present job or career development? I recommend using the feedback habit beyond work, for example with people who serve you in shops and cafes, or when you're travelling on business or on holiday.

PART FIVE

BEING ON THE RECEIVING END

A WORD ABOUT BEING ON THE RECEIVING END

Well, it wouldn't be a feedback book without some techniques, tools and tips on how to handle being on the receiving end of feedback, would it?

If regular feedback is what people want, in real time and two-way, then at some point soon you will be on the receiving end of someone's reactions to your behaviour. And those reactions may be positive or they may express a need for improvement. You might be expecting the feedback – or it may come as a complete surprise.

WARNING! Your feedback giver may be nowhere near as skilled as you are now (or are on your way to becoming). When you receive someone's feedback, be aware that it may not be as considered, clear and actionable as it could be. You'll need to use your own feedback conversational skills to keep the discussion on the right track. So this might be a good time to remind you that feedback is a gift. Stay curious and receptive and you too can benefit from it.

1. **RECEPTIVITY**
GET SWITCHED ON TO RECEIVE

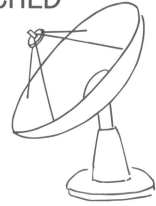

When someone gives you the gift of feedback, you need to be switched on to receive, so stay grounded in the here and now. That way you'll avert the so-called "amygdala hijack" when this tiny part of the brain, where our ancient fight–or–flight response lights up, perceives a threat and we can go on the attack or seek a quick exit.

Although we're no longer dodging sabre-toothed tigers, we still have fight–or–flight responses today, particularly at work. Remember that our neurological and physiological responses to criticism and perceived unfairness – psychological pain – can mirror those of physical pain. Being in fight–or–flight mode is no way to receive the gift of feedback.

You need to get grounded; that way you won't get carried away on a tide of emotions and stress hormones, and respond in ways that won't help anyone. Grounding is a technique that's great for keeping us present in the here and now. We often can react to perceived threats and potentially stressful situations with behaviours that have become habitual over time, but are no longer relevant or helpful.

Hand-in-hand with that, we can pay attention to our inner critic as it sounds off with its unhelpful soundtrack ("You'll never be any good at this!" "Who do you think you are?" or "It's not fair!"). When we're grounded, we're less likely to respond with an old script that was installed long ago. We're more likely to listen and respond with greater maturity and respect for the other person's contribution.

A practical grounding technique is to train yourself to focus very intently on what you can see, hear and feel, right here, right now. Pay close attention to your feedback giver's body language. Watch how this aligns with what the speaker is saying, listen carefully and, if it's appropriate, take notes, saying: *"I want to remember this as it's very valuable."* Notice how you're feeling, both sensations and emotions. Focus all your attention on the present situation.

EXERCISE

Practise staying grounded in everyday work conversations with colleagues, so when you next receive feedback you'll have mastered the art.
Tune out all other interference and focus intently on:

· What can you see around you?

  ....

  ....

- What sounds can you hear; are they soft or loud?

  ....

  ....

  ....

- What physical sensations are you feeling?

  ....

  ....

  ....

- What do you notice about the body language of the person you're with?

  ....

  ....

  ....

- What exactly does the speaker say and how do they say it?

  ....

  ....

2. **CLARITY**
GET SPECIFIC

Ideally your feedback giver will start the conversation on the right foot, saying something like, *"Can I give you some feedback?"* or *"Can we talk about how that meeting went?"*

If you weren't expecting any feedback, you may feel caught unaware – whether the feedback is positive or corrective – so remember to stay grounded. Check what prompted the feedback.

"It would really help to know what I said or did that prompted your feedback. Can you tell me more?"

"Please, can you elaborate on what I said or did that gave the impression I was (insert positive or negative adjective used here)?"
"Was this the only time you've noticed (the behaviour) or have there been others?"

By doing this, you're helping your feedback giver get to the first stage of **EDGE**: **E**xplaining your behaviour. If you're fortunate, your feedback giver will identify the action. It may take more questions to get clarity; make sure you hear them out.

Then you can move from cause to effect – **D**escribing the impact – and more of the details.

"What impact did you notice (of the behaviour)?"
"How did that (your action) affect the situation?"
"What effect has it (your behaviour) had?"

EXERCISE

- Try saying the example questions out loud in different ways by varying your tone, pace, pitch and volume.
- Notice what a difference it makes, even though the words stay the same.
- How would you feel if someone asked you those questions, in that tone, pace, pitch and volume?
- Adjust and fine-tune until you're sure your questions will be received positively.

If you're able to guide your feedback giver through the **E**xplain the action and **D**escribe the impact stages of the **EDGE** framework, it will help keep the conversation on the right track.

If the feedback makes sense to you – you deserve the praise or recognition, or need to work on improving an aspect of your performance – you can advance from there.

What if you don't agree with the feedback? Resist the temptation to rebuff it immediately. Ask questions to establish what happened. It's vital you're both clear; only then can you make progress. If the feedback is accurate and supported with evidence, accept it gracefully (and move on to the next chapter).

You may need to counter the feedback and give your account if it's inconsistent with your version of events. Avoid taking a hostile position; seek to understand your feedback giver's needs and interests. If agreement can't be reached, you may need a third person to mediate and give their input.

3. ADVANCE
MOVE FORWARD

You – and your feedback giver – are now clear on the behaviour that's prompted the feedback, and its impact. Your feedback giver may have **G**iven you the mic in the conversation, so that you can say what you'll do more or less of. Or you may need to request your turn to speak:

"I can see what you mean and I'd like to offer some suggestions."
"OK, I think I've got it. How about we agree on some steps to take?"

Now that you've got the mic, it's time to say what you'll do to move forward. If the feedback is positive, you might simply commit to repeating the behaviour more often, or you might seize the moment to ask for more opportunities. If the feedback is corrective, you need to commit to making improvements.

"I'll rehearse my next presentation so it will flow better and I'll be better prepared for questions."

"How about I sum up at the end of the next project meeting and write up who's doing what by when?"

"Next time I'll take care to check that I understand what the client's saying and not jump in with interruptions."

EXERCISE

Think of one aspect of your performance that you're happy with and another that you'd like to improve. Imagine two different situations at work in the near future.

1. Your manager has praised you for a job well done. What will you say in response to their feedback so that you advance?

   ....

   ....

   ....

2. Your manager has pointed out something you need to improve on. What will you say in response to their feedback so that you move forward and make improvements?

   ....

   ....

   ....

Once you've responded to the feedback and both of you are happy, you need to **E**nd the conversation on a positive note and show your commitment.

"Thanks for that feedback. It's really valuable to know how I'm doing."
"I appreciate you taking time to give me feedback so I can improve."
"That's so helpful, thank you. Is it OK with you if I ask for your feedback on how it goes next time?"

4. RECIPROCITY
ASK FOR IT

If you're really going to get the feedback habit, why wait? You need to start asking for feedback now. You never know, the feedback you get just might be really good! And if it's not? Better to know now than not know at all – or until it's too late.

The gift you'll get when you receive feedback is the chance to see yourself as others see you. It's better than looking at yourself in the mirror. Those little habits you didn't know you had, those things you say without noticing, the ways you do something well that you've been taking for granted – you'll be much more aware of what they are and how they impact others when you get feedback.

Who to ask?

- Your manager
- Your team, direct reports
- Clients and customers
- External contacts and suppliers
- Peers and colleagues
- Former managers and colleagues
- Your mentor or coach

Top tip: identify your "feedback friends" – a select group of people you can rely on to give you feedback that's considered, clear and actionable. Aim to have a mix of people from different disciplines and seniority levels. Don't be surprised if they ask you to respond in kind by giving them your feedback on how they're doing. Take that as a compliment on your feedback skills.

What about close friends, relatives and loved ones? I'd advise caution around this, particularly until you've mastered your own feedback skills – both giving and receiving. If your loved one's feedback is less than kind, a significant relationship could be damaged. Or their desire to avoid upsetting you may lead to feedback that's less than honest. Once you've mastered the art of giving and receiving the gift of feedback, you will be able to use it to enhance many relationships. That is possible through regular practice, reflection and learning as you progress. But remember, although your loved ones know you well, they may not be as skilled at giving the gift of feedback as you are.

EXERCISE

Who will you ask? Identify two or three different people you trust to give you clear feedback at work.

1. ....

2. ....

3. ....

How to ask? That's in the next section.

5. FRAMING
HELP OTHERS
TO BE HELPFUL

HELP THEM TO HELP YOU

What do you want to receive feedback about? It's important to be specific. Asking a colleague, "Could you give me some feedback please?" could cause discomfort for them and might start a very different conversation to the one you'd hoped to have.

It's better to be clear and help them to help you by asking for feedback in advance, and carefully framing what you would like them to focus on. This will save you both time and effort later, as they won't be fumbling for answers to your questions about how you did, or worse, giving you vague comments. Instead, when you frame the feedback you seek, you'll be helping someone to give you an **EDGE**.

Your feedback giver will need to know what's prompted you to ask for their input rather than anyone else's. Explaining this can be the simplest way for you to start the conversation. For example:

"Can you help me? As someone who's good at it I'd like your feedback on how I do at the next presentation."
"I need some feedback about how I run this project, and know I can trust you to be honest."
"I really want to get better at speaking up in meetings. Since you've raised this as something I need to work on, can you give me some feedback after the next client meeting?"

"Would you give me some feedback after this conference call? I'm working on asking the right questions and it would be a great help to hear your observations."

If your chosen feedback giver agrees, you can then get more specific. For example:

"The most useful thing for me would be to hear how I interact with the audience."

"Please give me your thoughts on how I communicate with people on the project to keep everyone informed."

"It would be great to hear what impact you think it has on the meeting when I speak up."

"Which questions were more productive in getting to the heart of the matter?"

EXERCISE

Identify three aspects of your work on which you want feedback and why:

1. ....

2. ....

3. ....

How will you ask your chosen feedback giver and help them to help you?

....

6. **PERSPECTIVE**
GETTING 360-DEGREE FEEDBACK

Many organizations operate a system of 360-degree or multi-rater feedback. The aim here is to offer 10 suggestions for receiving 360-degree feedback on your performance.

1. Establish up front what the ground rules are in your organization. Are raters anonymous or attributed? Who gets to see your 360?

2. Accept that multiple perspectives give a more rounded view of how others see us. This is usually fairer than just one person's point of view.

3. Seek advice from colleagues who have more experience of how the system works.

4. Receiving this type of feedback can feel threatening – after all, you're outnumbered – so beware the fight-or-flight response. Remember to stay grounded in the here and now.

5. Appreciate that other people's opinions are just that – and they're entitled to them. Look for common themes, whether positive or corrective.

6. Celebrate the positive feedback!

7. If critical comments are consistent, pay attention to when and how you're falling short. Devise an action plan to improve your performance.

8. Seek clarification if feedback is in any way unclear.

9. Ensure you have the opportunity to follow up with someone once you've had time to digest the feedback. This could be your line manager, department head, someone in HR – or a mix.

10. Raise your self-awareness; 360-degree feedback can be eye-opening. Different people see different aspects of you – which you may have been unaware of.

EXERCISE

Look back at your last 360-degree review. Highlight the feedback about your performance that you were already aware of.

....

Use a different colour to highlight aspects of your performance that you were unaware of until the feedback.

....

7. **PROTECTION**
HANDLING FEEDBACK ON YOUR TEAM

When you get feedback from leaders, your peers and other colleagues about your team members – whether the comments are positive or negative – the **EDGE** principles apply. You need to identify the actions that have prompted the feedback, as well as its impact, and move the conversation to a positive resolution.

This is particularly important if you weren't there when the praise-worthy or poor behaviour happened. In a typical matrix organization, this is often the case. Your team members need to know they can trust you to pass on praise and to have their back if they come in for criticism.

Here are some DOs and DON'Ts when someone offers their feedback on one member, some or all of your team:

DO
- Get the context: ask when this happened and who was there.
- Ask questions to identify the action that prompted the feedback.
- Ask the person what they saw and heard – get specific and nail the detail.
- Make notes.
- Check if the behaviour was a one-off or is a frequent occurrence.
- Establish whether the feedback-giver spoke with your team member at the time, and if so what was said (maybe they said "great job" and simply want you to be aware of it).
- Ask their advice if you think it's appropriate.
- Seek corroboration if the feedback has serious implications.
- Thank the giver of feedback.
- Follow up with them once you've had a conversation with your team member(s).

DON'T
- Perceive any feedback on "my people" as a blatant territorial breach, grow a pair of horns and charge at the feedback-giver with counter-accusations about their team.
- Rebuff any praise with "Well it IS their job after all!"
- Tell the feedback giver that if you ever want their opinion you'll ask for it.
- Interrupt your feedback giver; it may have taken considerable thought about whether to approach you and what to say.

If you were present during the event that prompted the feedback, you'll most likely be aware of the action in question. This makes life much simpler; you'll be guiding the conversation wherever possible to ensure you're clear about the feedback-giver's take on the behaviour and its impact. If the feedback is positive, be sure to relay it to your team. If the feedback is seeking a behaviour change or course correction from one member or some of your team, reach agreement about the steps to be taken and who will be responsible. Follow up with the feedback-giver to check on progress.

EXERCISE

Make a list of the people on whom you can rely to give considered, clear and actionable feedback about your immediate team.

....

....

....

....

....

....

....

....

8. **EXPLORATION**
UNCHARTED TERRITORY

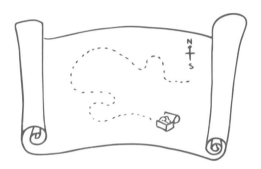

Most of us can get defensive when someone criticizes something about ourselves – it's hardwired. Yet at the same time, many of us have a critical inner editor that can drown out praise. Obviously both factors come into play when we're on the receiving end of feedback from others.

- We can brush off praise for something that comes easily to us – and it may be a strength we've been taking for granted.
- We can be falsely modest when praised, when we should be thanking the giver and figuring out how and when we'll do more of what got us noticed in a good way.
- We can be selective about what feedback we'll give credence to – whether that's because of the giver, how the feedback aligns with our opinion of ourselves, or the degree of difficulty and risk in acting on it.

So what?

This is why feedback is so valuable. Our self-awareness can usually do with some external input and validation. Every one of us can benefit from exploring the often-uncharted territory that is the person who shows up when we're around.

EXERCISE

1. Make a note of what you believe are your top five strengths and your top five weaknesses

    Strengths   Weaknesses

    ....

    ....

    ....

    ....

    ....

2. Check your self-assessment against others' feedback about your performance. Look for comments that corroborate and disprove your point of view.

    ....

3. What insights have you gained?

    ....

---

9. **GRATITUDE**
GOOD
FEEDBACK
IS A GIFT

Is feedback a gift? When it's badly done, poorly considered, vague and yet judgmental of the recipient, obviously not – or at least it's not a gift that benefits the person on the receiving end. It's of no use to the recipient and if anything, makes working relationships worse. Maybe it's like a novelty gift in bad taste – it's remembered for all the wrong reasons after it's been discarded.

When feedback is done well and it's considered, clear and action-able, given in a conversation not a monologue, then it really can be a gift, and one that should be valued.

When you give colleagues an **EDGE**, whether it's positive or corrective, you'll be giving them a gift that will serve them well as they progress in their careers. The same goes for you when you get feedback from others. When you go a step further and actively ask for feedback, you are purposefully putting yourself on the receiving end by asking for something that is within their ability to provide.

I've referred to the cocktail of thoughts and feelings that we can all experience when we receive feedback, from sheer panic to serene curiosity. But something I can't stress enough is the need to feel and show gratitude when we are given feedback. Even if the feed-back is tough to hear, the giver's underlying belief is usually that we will ultimately benefit from the feedback and when we apply it we will improve. For this you need to be grateful.

What's more, the further you progress in your career, the harder it can be to get feedback; people are wary of telling you like it is, as it may seem disrespectful of your position. So those who do speak up and contribute feedback are especially worthy of your gratitude. If you're switched on to receive feedback, you are far less likely to become one of the "poor managers" cited by the aforementioned Investors in People survey's respondents as the main reason for their unhappiness at work.

How can you show gratitude to people who give you feedback?

- Say "thank you" next time you see them.
- Write them a personal note.
- Give them a call.
- Tell them the effect the feedback has had.
- Praise their feedback skills on social media.
- Tell their manager what a difference the feedback has made.

EXERCISE

Brainstorm all the ways you will show gratitude to the people who have recently given you feedback, whether it was positive or corrective.

....

10. GET THE HABIT
SPOTTING
OPPORTUNITIES
FOR
FEEDBACK

There are more opportunities than you might think for you to ask someone else for the gift of their feedback; several might present themselves in a single working day.

- Refer back to the aspects of your performance about which you want some feedback from colleagues.
- Take a good look at your calendar for the next three weeks and identify the opportunities for your colleagues to give you feedback on whatever aspect is most appropriate for the situation and their input.
- Now you can add some calendar reminders to ask your colleagues for feedback ahead of time so they're ready to give you an **EDGE**.

VERBS CHEAT SHEET

The aims of this cheat sheet are to:

- Help you give feedback that's clear and nonjudgmental by focusing on actions.
- Encourage you to broaden your repertoire of verbs when discussing your own and others' behaviour.

Adapt	Build	Decide	Engage
Advise	Call	Defend	Evaluate
Adjust	Challenge	Define	Examine
Agree	Change	Delegate	Experiment
Analyse	Check	Demonstrate	Explain
Answer	Choose	Describe	Explore
Apply	Coach	Design	Extend
Argue	Collaborate	Determine	Fiddle
Arrive	Communicate	Develop	Find
Articulate	Compile	Devise	Finish
Ask	Complete	Discuss	Focus
Assign	Contribute	Dispute	Forgo
Balance	Convince	Distinguish	Form
Bargain	Create	Draft	Generate
Begin	Critique	Draw	Give examples
Break	Debate	Empathize	Give feedback

Grasp	Locate	Project	Simplify
Group	Make	Prove	Solve
Haggle	Manage	Question	Sort
Hear	Mark	Rate	Speak
Hypothesize	Measure	Raise	Specify
Identify	Modify	Reach	State
Illustrate	Move	Read	Stop
Imply	Negotiate	Refer	Suggest
Improve	Note	Reflect	Summarize
Influence	Observe	Relate	Support
Inform	Order	Repeat	Talk
Inspect	Organise	Report	Teach
Integrate	Outline	Reply	Tell
Interpret	Participate	Request	Track
Interrupt	Perform	Resolve	Train
Introduce	Persuade	Respond	Turn
Invent	Plan	Review	Uncover
Investigate	Play	Revise	Use
Justify	Practise	Run	Verify
Keep records	Praise	Search	Wait
Laugh	Predict	Select	Walk
Link	Prepare	Share	Welcome
List	Present	Shout	Whisper
Listen	Produce	Show	Write

This list is by no means exhaustive. If you have any suggestions for verbs that can be added, please email them to **hello@zoomly.co.uk**

ACKNOWLEDGEMENTS

Thanks to the many participants on training workshops I've run over the years – your feedback continues to keep me on my toes and constantly learning.

Thanks to Martin, Sara and the LID team for their ideas, expertise – and patience.

Sincere thanks to Kevin Duncan for generously giving expert advice, guidance and support.

Finally, thanks to Chris and my parents for your encouragement, listening to my endless wittering about 'the book' as it progressed.

ABOUT THE AUTHOR

DAWN SILLETT is a management trainer, coach and author. After working in the advertising industry in the UK and overseas for 15 years, she switched careers and now works with employers large and small to improve individual, team and business performance.

**CONTACT THE AUTHOR FOR ADVICE,
TRAINING, COACHING AND FACILITATING**

**dawn@zoomly.co.uk
thefeedbackbook.com**

ALSO BY THE AUTHOR:
How to be Zoomly at Work

RESOURCES AND FURTHER READING

1. Accenture's "Goodbye Annual Performance Appraisals" article can be accessed via their company newsroom https://newsroom.accenture.com/news/goodbye-annual-performance-appraisals.htm

2. Chartered Institute of Personnel and Development (CIPD), Employee Outlook, Autumn 2014. Accessible via the CIPD's site: www.cipd.co.uk

3. Investors in People (IiP), Job Exodus Trends. Accessible via IiP's site: https://www.investorsinpeople.com/jobexodus2016

4. *Positivity* by Barbara Fredrickson, published by Oneworld Publications (2009) is available on Amazon.

5. 'WORK STRESS AND HEALTH: the Whitehall II study' Published by Public and Commercial Services Union on behalf of Council of Civil Service Unions/Cabinet Office can be accessed via UCL https://www.ucl.ac.uk/whitehallII/pdf/wii-bookletST